Words by Katy Pike
Pictures by Luke Jurevicius

X as in fox

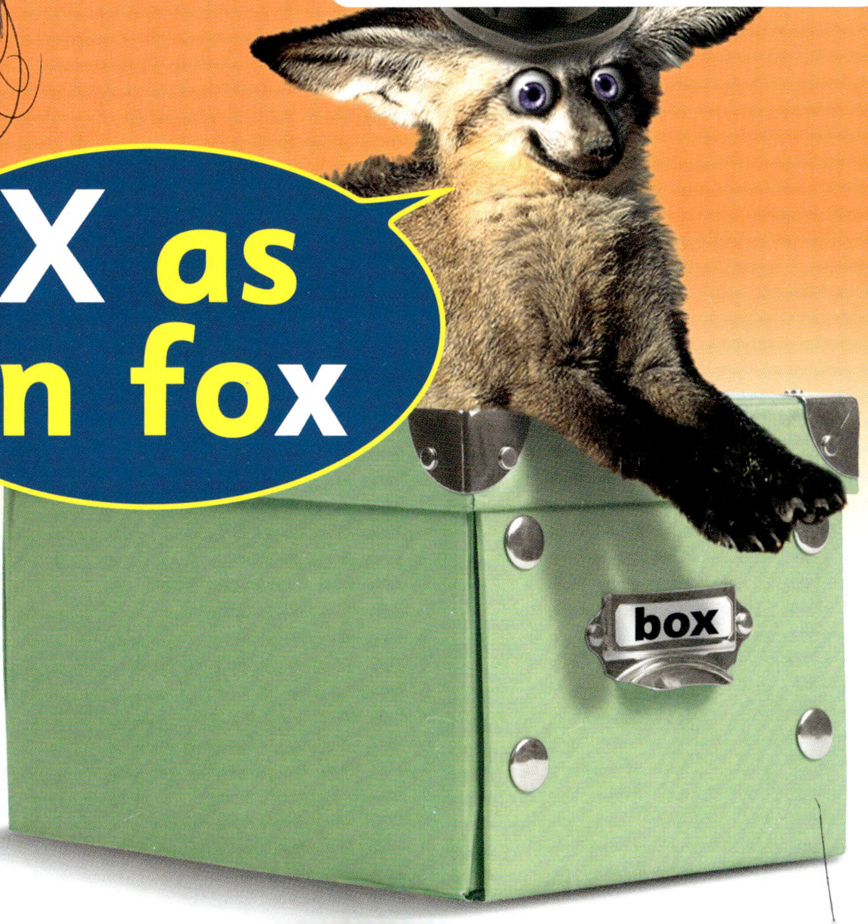

Fox

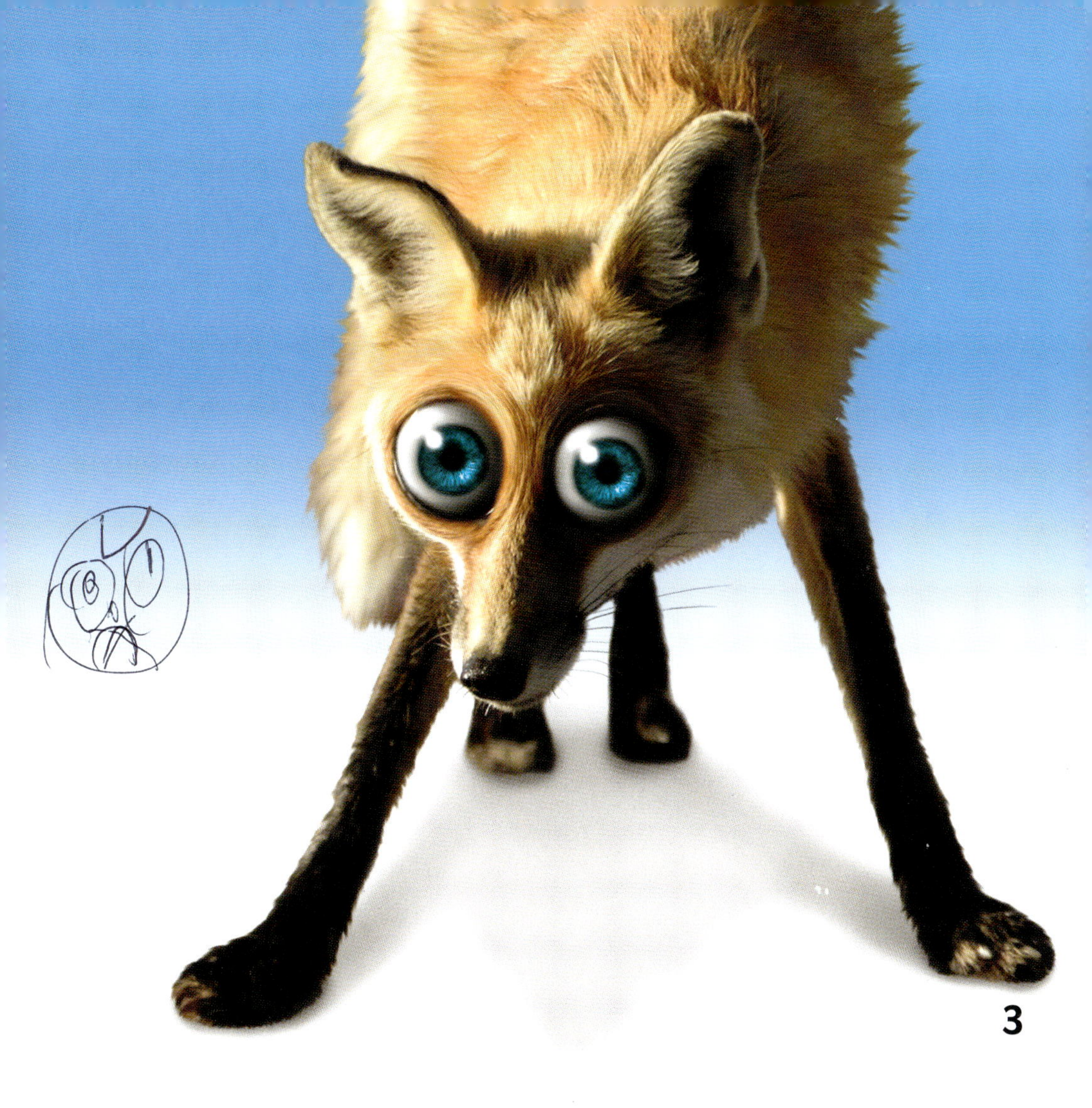

B ox

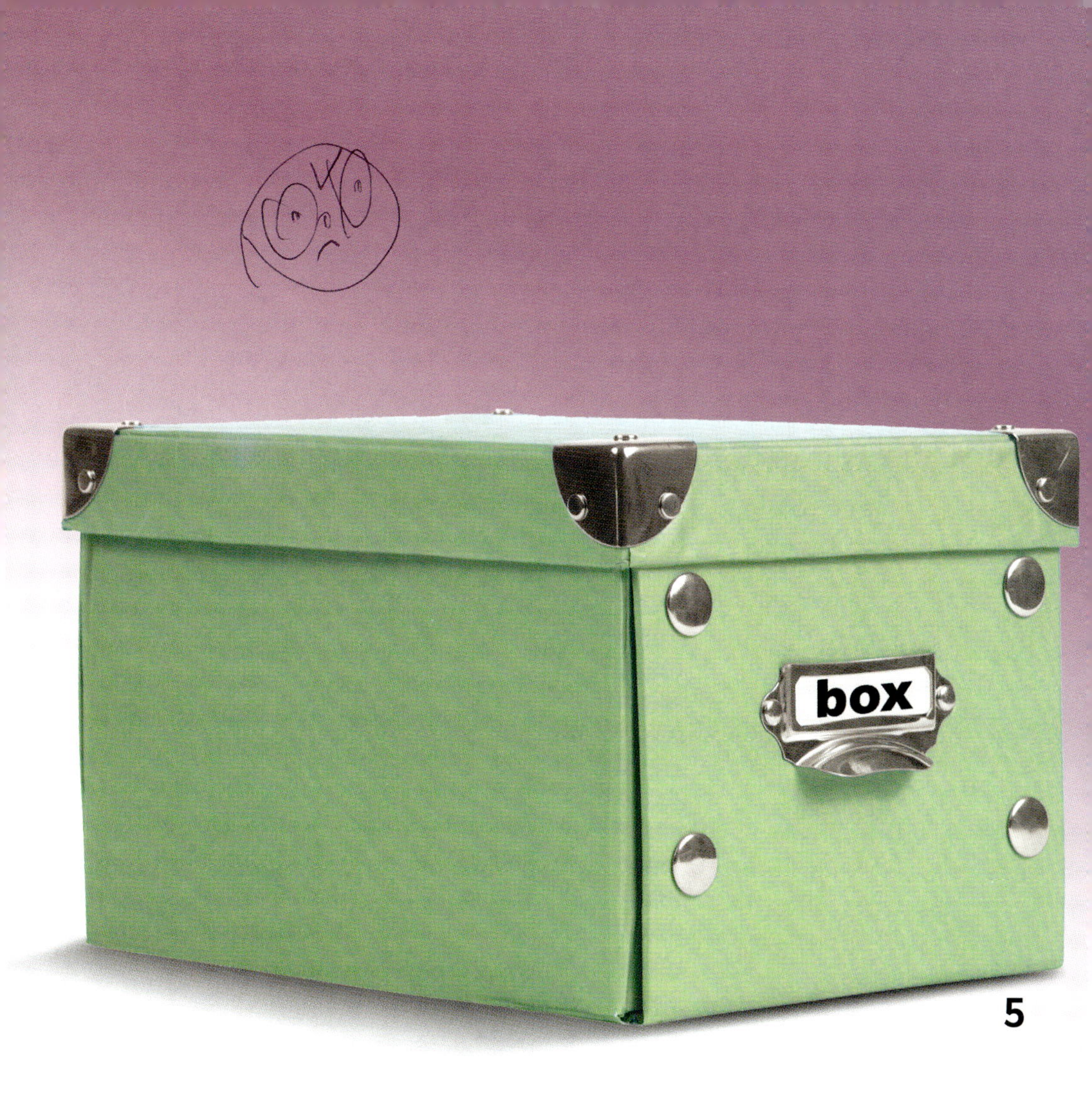
box

A fox in a box

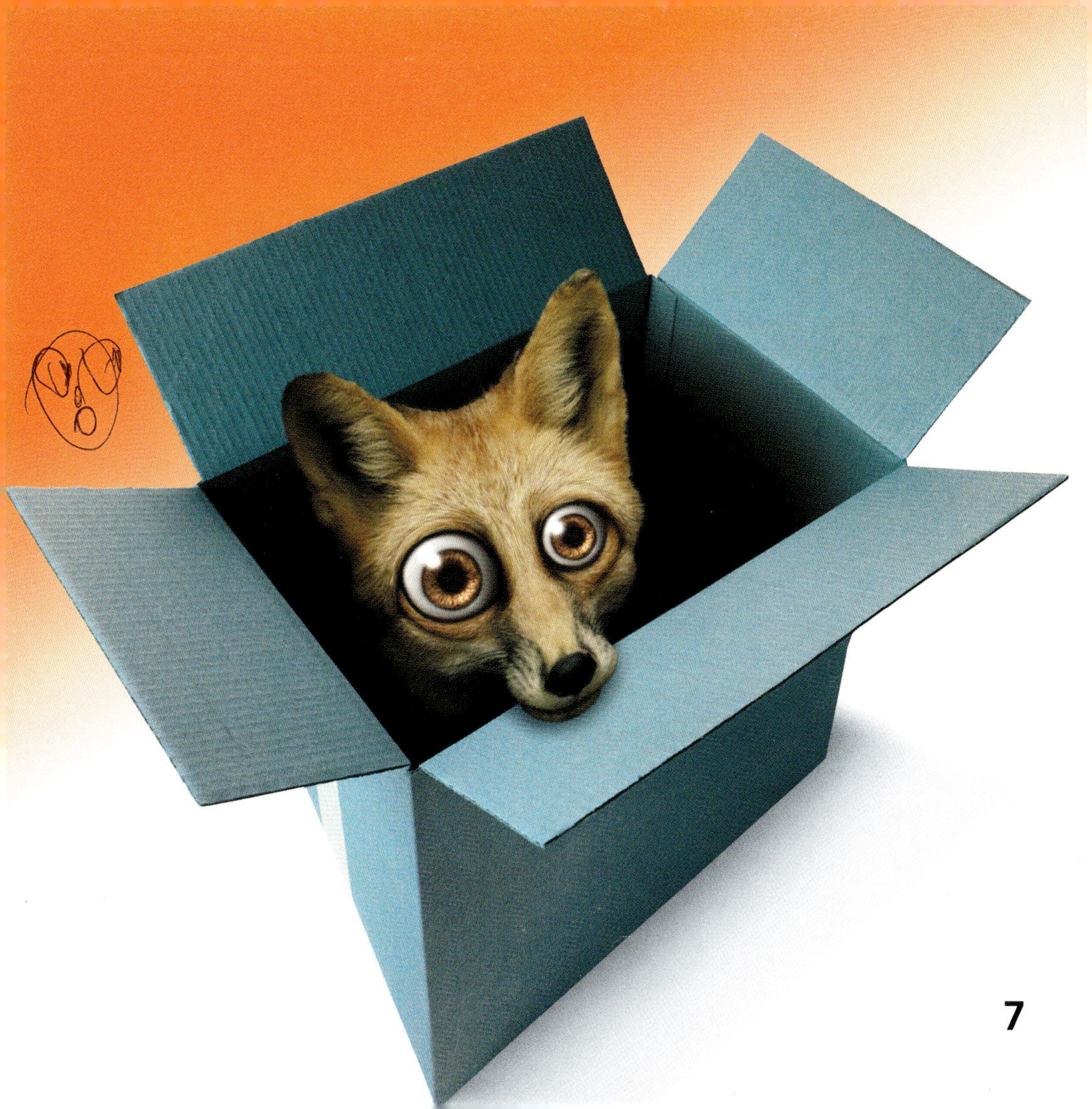

Six foxes

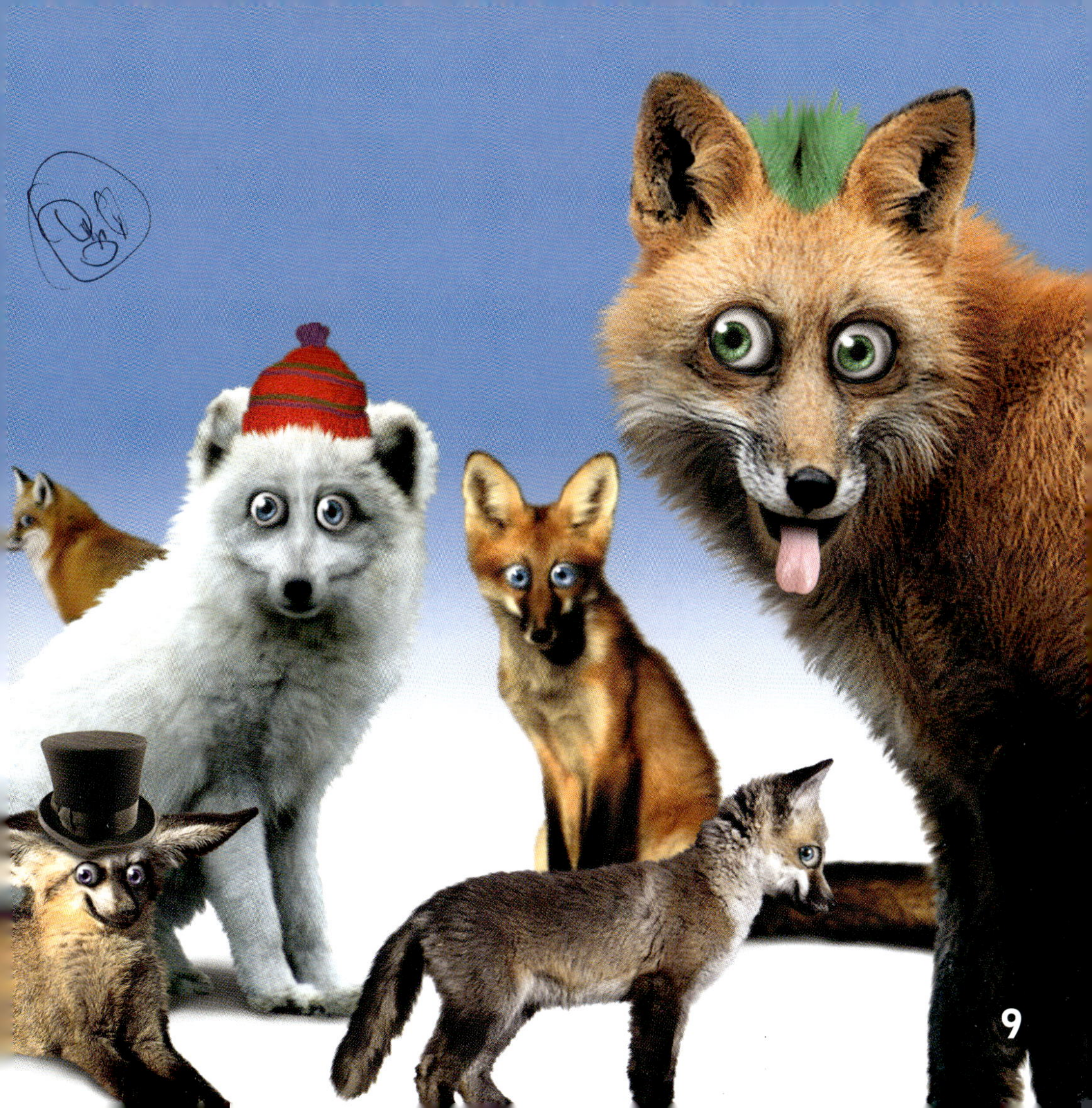

Six boxes

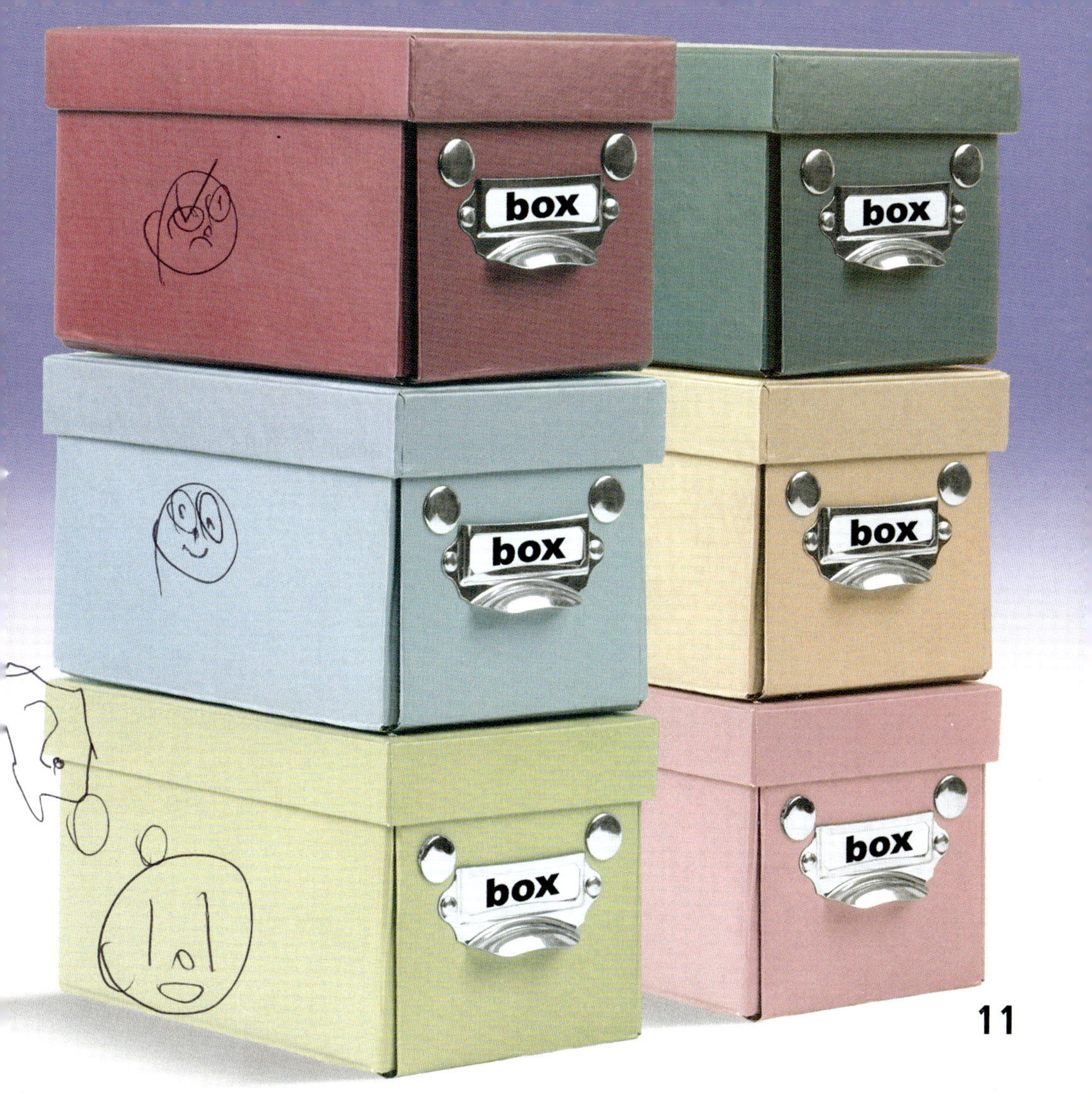
box
box
box
box
box
box

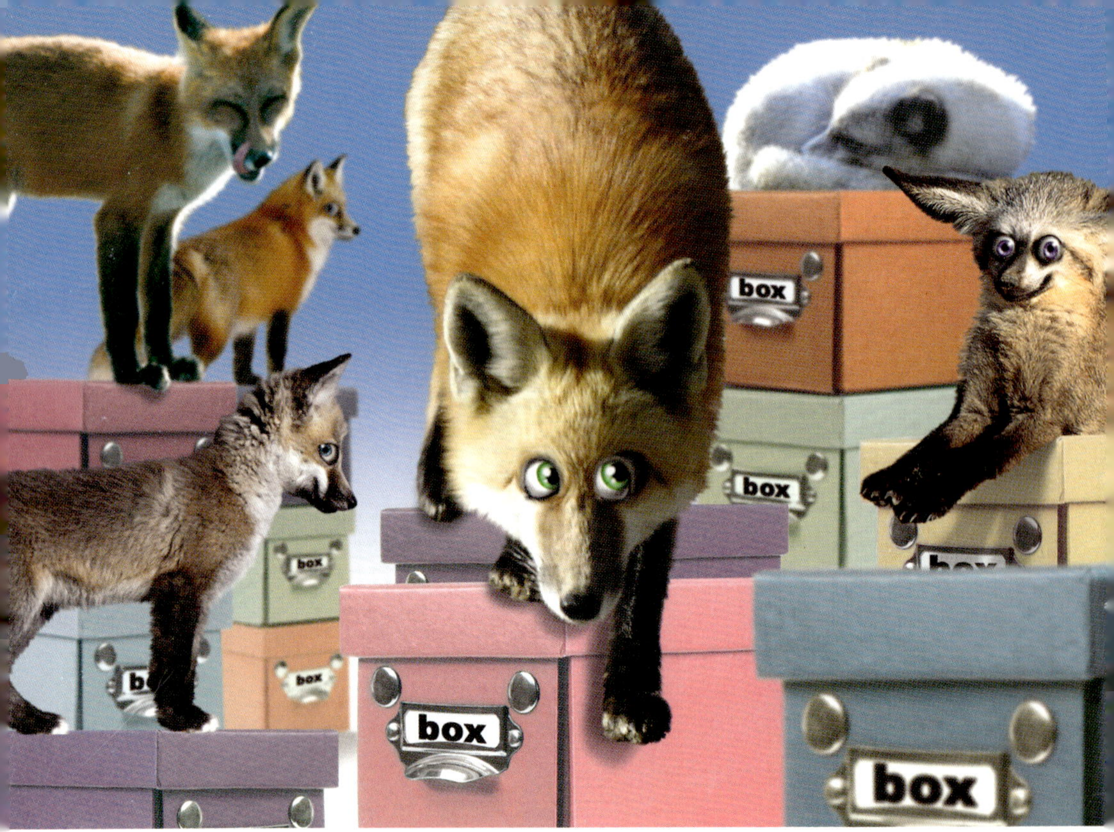

Six foxes on boxes